The Adventures of Scuba Jack
Copyright 2020 by Beth Costanzo

Cheetahs are the fastest land animal reaching up to 69.5 miles an hour in just three seconds! Their bodies are made for speed with their long legs and spine, claws to grip the ground and long tail for steering and balance. Cheetahs are carnivores so they live off animals they find in the African plains. The Cheetah's great eyesight helps it find its prey during the day. These animals include gazelles, warthogs, rabbits, and birds. If cheetahs are hunting in groups, they can hunt bigger animals like wildebeest and zebras. Cheetahs hunt during the day to avoid competition from other powerful predators like lions, leopards, and hyenas.

The Adventures
of
SCUBA JACK

Cheetahs have a pale yellow coat with black dots. Every cheetah has a different pattern of spots. A fully grown cheetah can have 2,000 to 3,000 spots on its body! Their pattern of spots help them camouflage while hunting. Their prey will be unable to see them while the cheetah slowly creeps up on them. Then the cheetah will chase it, knock the prey to the ground and bite it in the neck. Cheetahs are only able to chase their prey for only 20 to 30 seconds.

The Adventures
of
SCUBA JACK

Did you know that cheetahs are the only big cats that can't roar? They will let out a chirping noise if they feel threatened and they will make a purring sound if they are happy. Cheetahs weigh from 77 to 143 pounds and are 3.5 to 4.5 feet tall. With their tail being over 2 feet long. Cheetahs usually travel in packs that consist of the mother, her cubs and siblings. Or, males cheetahs will join with them for hunting. Female cheetahs will give birth to two to eight cubs in one litter. The cubs will stay with their mother for 16 to 24 months or until they are able to hunt for themselves. Cheetahs lifespan in the wild is 10 to 12 years.

The Adventures
of
SCUBA JACK

CHEETAH ACTIVITIES

Trace then rewrite the phrase below.

Who is the fastest land animal?

A.Jaguar

B.Cheetah

C. Hyena

What is a cheetah's maximum speed?

What does a cheetah's tail help with?

Cheetahs are Herbivores, Omnivores or Carnivores?

Count the cheetahs then circle the answer.

4 5 6	6 7 8
6 5 7	7 9 8

The Adventures
of
SCUBA JACK

WHAT COMES NEXT?

CHOOSE THE RIGHT ANSWER

 9 8 7

 8 4 6

 6 7 9

 2 6 4

 2 3 4

 6 2 4

CONNECT THE DOTS

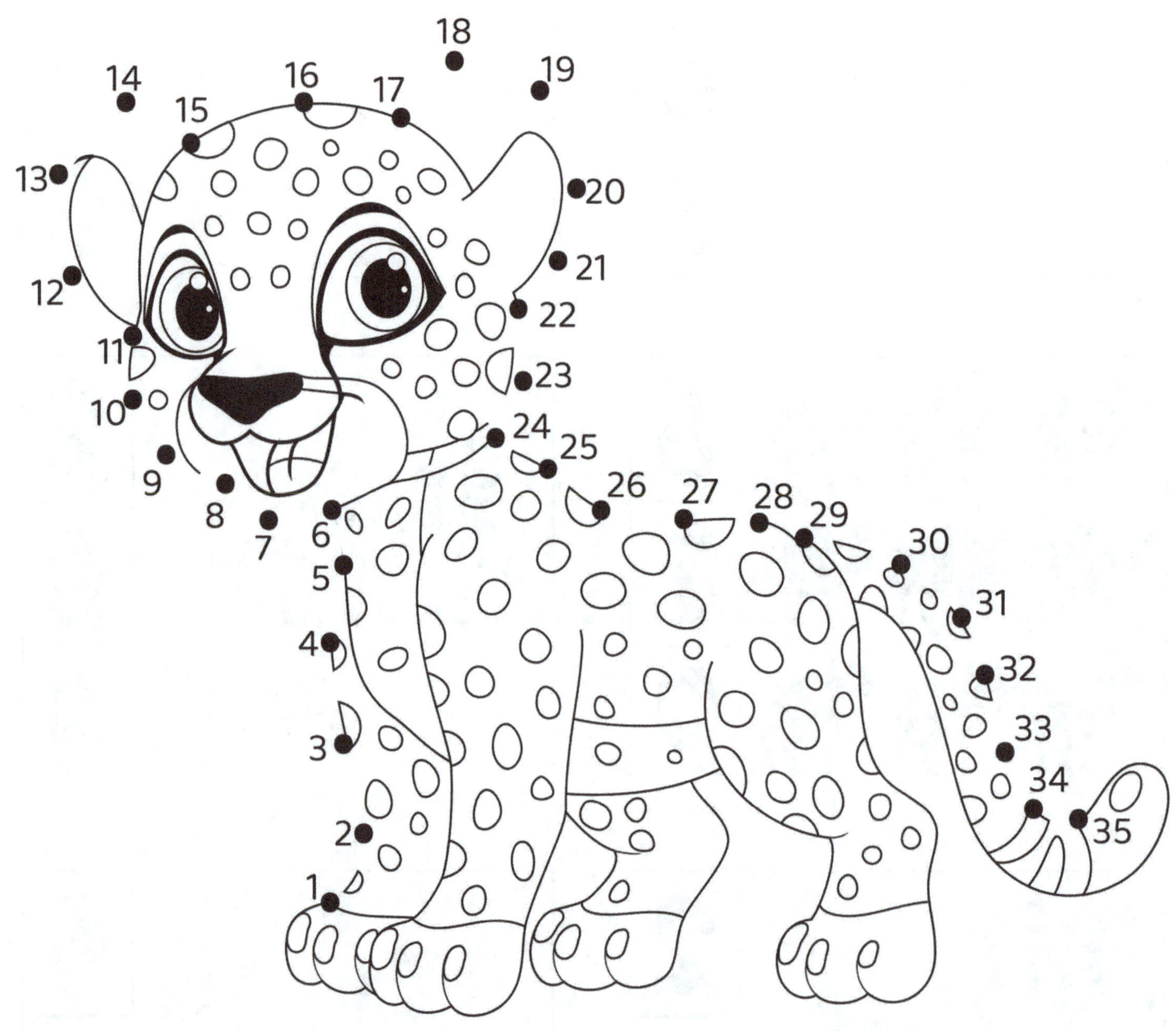

WORD SEARCH

Find and circle the words listed below.

O	H	B	I	R	D	D	U	S	P
T	L	I	O	N	S	R	O	A	R
K	U	D	M	W	C	R	O	O	E
D	W	R	O	Y	U	E	A	B	Y
C	A	M	O	U	F	L	A	G	E
W	R	O	A	R	P	C	M	O	X
H	W	C	B	C	E	H	H	U	E
A	G	N	U	T	M	E	I	L	A
L	V	O	C	H	E	E	T	A	H
Z	E	B	R	A	A	L	M	O	N

Cub   Roar   Cheetah   Prey

Lion   Camouflage   Zebra

COLOR IT

Cheetah Craft

1- Cut out the Cheetah Parts
2- Glue the head to the body
3- Glue tail to the back of the body
4- Color your Cheetah & Add black dotted pattern!

The Adventures
of
SCUBA JACK

Visit us at:

www.adventuresofscubajack.com